HOW A WINNER THINKS

Motivational Tips For Girls!

Grace-Frances Afful

Copyright © 2021 Grace-Frances Afful.

All rights reserved. This book or any portion thereof may not be reproduced or used in any manner whatsoever without the express written permission of the publisher except for the use of brief quotations in a book review.

For permissions contact:

gracefrancesafful@gmail.com

Share with Friends!

Write a review!

After reading this book, please take the time to write an honest review on Amazon.com. These reviews will help me to master my craft.

Please feel free to email me at gracefrancesafful@gmail.com or check out my website at www.gracefrancesafful.com

Table of Contents

Introduction 5

Tip 1: Commit to Your Goals 7

Tip 2: Perseverance - How To Develop It 10

Tip 3: Surround Yourself With Like- Minded People 14

Tip 4: Listen To Your Parents Or Guardians 17

Tip 5: What Can Self-Love Do for You? 20

Tip 6: Dealing With Procrastination 23

Tip 7: Dealing With Self-Doubt 25

Tip 8: What Can You Learn From Successful People? .. 29

Tip 9: Keep Your Mind Open to Positive Change 32

Conclusion 34

Introduction

So you have finally decided to be the winner you were born to be! As you begin to be more aware of who you truly are, winning will be the next thing that will begin to chase you down.

Every successful teenage girl carries a winning mindset.

If you have the will to win, you are on the road to success. Girls who are willing to overcome obstacles are those with a winning attitude. For them, winning is not an option it is a must.

As a teen and upcoming adult, learn not to talk and walk in defeat. There have been times in your life when you lost hope. Just because you did not do as well as expected at whatever task does not make you a loser. How about facing that challenge with a better attitude?

No one is defeated until they first entertain and then accept the defeated thought. Winning and defeat cannot coexist. You either think as a winner or as a loser. Winners never quit and quitters never win.

Here are some quotes on winning — please read them carefully:

- "A winner is someone who recognizes his God-given talents, works his tail off to develop them into skills and uses these skills to accomplish his goals." -Larry Bird.

- "For me, life is continuously being hungry. The meaning of life is not simply to exist, to survive, but to move ahead, to go up, to achieve, to conquer." -Arnold Schwarzenegger.

- "A winner commits. A loser makes a lot of promises. People who stick through thick and thin times are the winners." -Laura Lyseight.

- "A winner is a dreamer who never gives up" -Nelson Mandela

Tip 1:

Commit to Your Goals

"Commitment is the foundation of great accomplishments."

- Heidi Reeder

Tennis legend Arthur Ashe once said, "Success is a journey." Just as a physical journey requires a destination, so does a journey for success require a goal, which is that ultimate desire that you hope to achieve. While a goal is important to success, we must also bear in mind that we cannot achieve a goal unless we are committed to the journey.

Imagine it is the beginning of the year. You sit down to write your resolutions or goals. You work on what you want for the year. Then you develop a plan to get you to your goals. Mid-year comes around and you realize that you are still working on a few goals but have completely forgotten about three goals you wrote down. So what happened? At the time you wrote the goals, you were committed to them. Why did you stop working on them? It was your level of commitment.

Growing up, when I was the age of six, my uncle taught me how to ride a bike without training wheels. I must emphasize that it was difficult in the beginning. I fell so many times and awarded myself a lot of scratches. Every day, my uncle and I went outside so I could practice riding my bike. One day, he pushed me on the bike, and I started pedaling without falling! I was slowly learning how to ride without training wheels! Eventually, I could ride without assistance! My uncle and I were committed to the goal of having me ride a bike without training wheels.

Commitment is a very powerful and crucial part of following through and accomplishing goals. Let's look at a few examples. Before we leave for school, we take a shower because we are committed to good personal hygeine. If your goal is to be on honor roll, you commit yourself to studying and to doing the very best you can.

In setting goals, it is important to identify the category under which they fall. For example, your goal may be to work out to stay in shape. This goal would go under the category of Physical Health. On the other hand, your goal might be to save as much money as you can during the school year. This is the first step in the process, identifying what you are committed to working on.

Next, decide if it is a goal you would want to commit to for the long haul. To help with this process ask yourself these three questions:

1. How clear am I about this goal?
2. Is it something I am willing to write down and take responsibility for?

3. Can I picture myself achieving this?

How clear am I about this goal? Answering this question will help you gain clarity on what it is you are working towards. Part of this question is to see where you are starting. Ask yourself on a scale of 0-100%, just how clear am I? If you can get clear about your goal, you will be more committed to it.

Is it something I am willing to write down and take responsibility for? According to Rebecca Temsen in an article named "The Psychology of Writing Down Goals," our dreams come true more easily and faster when we write them down. When we write down our goals, we are more likely to work towards achieving them. It is also good to read over your goals daily. Read them out clearly to yourself so you can stay connected to them.

Can I picture myself achieving this? Again, ask yourself on a scale of 0-100%, how clear is your goal? The clearer your goal is to you, the more committed you will be to achieving it. For example, if you want to make a YouTube channel, see yourself putting out amazing content on YouTube. If you want to make a YouTube channel, think of a name, think of a theme, and see yourself as a successful YouTuber. To take this a step further, you can plan out your content on a vision board.

The next time you make a list of your goals, try these steps. Decide what area you want to work on. Identify what you want to achieve in this area. Clarify exactly what it is you want. Decide if you are willing to write it down and take responsibility for it. Picture yourself achieving your goal, then develop it further in your mind. Make the picture big and colorful. Committing to this process is a sure way to create exactly what you desire!

Tip 2:

Perseverance - How To Develop It

"A little progress each day adds up to big results."

- Satya Nanyi

Perseverance is essential if one is to realize their goals and achieve success. It is the act of persisting to do something despite challenges, obstacles, and disappointments.

From my experience in pursuing academic excellence and athletics, I have learned personally that with perseverance, challenges can be overcome.

Unfortunately, many people rob themselves of success because they do not have the perseverance to see their goals through.

However, developing perseverance requires effort on one's part.

Perseverance Requires Faith and Belief

To develop perseverance in everyday life, you will have to believe that you can actually succeed and meet your goals.

This belief that you can succeed will be the motivation that will push you to strive towards your goal regardless of what obstacles you come up against.

On the other hand, if you don't have the belief that you can accomplish a particular goal, then you are more likely to quit and leave your dreams behind you.

I attended private school from preschool to 4th grade. From 5th grade onwards, I have attended public school. Making that switch from private to public school was very difficult for me because the learning environment is so different. I was used to smaller class sizes as well as being able to engage with my teachers often. When I switched to public school in 5th grade, I realized very quickly that I could not ask all the questions I had because there were a lot more students in the classroom. My grades started dropping, and I was very devastated. I complained constantly about school because I felt that I was trying my hardest, and it just wasn't enough. However, I continued to work hard. The truth is I did not even realize that I was adapting to my new environment and slowly improving. I received my first Honor Roll certificate in public school and was very happy because my perseverance had paid off. It did not stop there. Every time I have wanted to give up, I have reflected on my experience in transitioning from private to public school and continued to persevere.

Yes, you may encounter major challenges or possibly failures along the way, but with perseverance you will eventually succeed. Not giving up easily will allow you to revise your game-plan, tweak your strategies, and keep moving forward and in the process, improve your chances of success.

So, your ability to persevere is part of the process of achieving success.

What things can you do to develop perseverance in life?

1. First, you must establish what it is you truly desire. What goal do you really want to achieve?

2. Have a clear step-by-step plan of how you're going to achieve your goal. Your plan is your roadmap to your desired destination. Without one, you'll get lost.

3. 3. Before you pursue a goal, commit yourself to work towards it for a specific period and do not give up. Make this period as long or as short as you want but the important thing is not to quit before the specified time. Revising your strategies is fine, but quitting is fatal. Quitting will only show your inability to persevere and see things through.

4. Identify potential obstacles you could face along the way. This will not only prepare you mentally but will also help you to identify alternative strategies and plans.

5. Seek out help and moral support from family, friends, or mentors. They will help keep you focused and motivated on following through until you achieve your goal.

6. Self-control is a must when developing perseverance in daily life. Exercising self-control ensures you remain focused on the task or tasks at hand and not get side-tracked. Making deliberate efforts

to study with no distractions, such as cell phones, after-school is an example of self-control.

7. Establish consistent daily habits. A daily habit could be writing in a planner to remain organized. Setting alarms to do a specific task at a specific time could also help. Taking small steps of progress consistently every day will mean that your efforts will compound and success will be inevitable.

8. The importance of perseverance in life cannot be stressed enough. To achieve any notable goal or success, then you must have the stamina to stay the course.

If perseverance is something you lack, then by following the tips above and applying a minimal amount of effort, you will soon realize that nothing is beyond your reach.

Tip 3:

Surround Yourself With Like-Minded People

"There are ways to meet people and surround yourself with like-minded people who will support you."

- Chris Colfer

One bit of advice I hear on a daily basis is "be careful who you hang around with." This advice has come from both my parents and almost all their friends. People who have advised me about the company I keep have done so with a sense of urgency. This is because their own life experiences have taught them the value of positive relationships.

I don't know if you've heard this statement, "You become like the people you associate with." I have three friends and a cousin who have good qualities that I admire. Their names are Mikayla, Jemimah, Keziah, and Rena.

Mikayla is very caring. She takes the time to listen. She goes the extra mile to help and is all in all considerate.

Jemimah is a good listener, a good friend, and a very purposeful person. She never gives up and is very persistent with her goals.

Keziah pays attention to details. She is courageous and does not walk away from challenges. She never lets her fears overcome her.

Rena is also a good listener and has a good sense of humor. She goes the extra mile for others. She is also very knowledgeable and uses her experiences to educate me.

All this to say that having hard-working and caring friends will change you for the better.

No matter how much you want to accomplish, no matter how big your dreams, no matter how motivated you are, you still need to be around like-minded people whose influence will positively impact your life.

If you are around people who have a carefree attitude towards their studies, make poor choices, and exhibit negative behavior, it is more likely that you will become like them. Who you keep in your space is very crucial to becoming a winner. Having people who do not have the same mindset as you is like poison which eventually destroys. Negative people downplay what is important to you and your journey as a winner. They often say, "No, you can't do that" or "No, you shouldn't." Instead, stay clear of them and be focused on your goals.

Let's remember that successful people surround themselves with successful people. Have you got a successful team? Who do you surround yourself with?

Surround yourself with people who have poised themselves to be successful and to win.

Tip 4:

Listen To Your Parents Or Guardians

"Respecting your parents is good, but honoring your parents is the best."

- Anne Grace

As teenage girls, we are more likely to listen to our friends than we are to our parents because we think that our parents belong to a different generation and have a different set of ideas. While this may be the case, their experiences can help guide us through life. Have you ever thought that your parents did not understand your generation? I can definitely relate to that view, but I could also talk about several instances where they were proved right. What I lack is their experience. In hindsight, I have learned that our parents will always have our welfare at heart and will want us to succeed. It is very important to listen to the guidance they give.

How Teens Can Learn Respect

1. Don't get upset when your parents give you a consequence for your actions. Respect your parents. Don't pout, stomp your feet, slam a door, or raise your voice in anger. Remain calm and discuss the situation in a rational manner.

2. Make conscious choices. Think before you act. Pause before you speak or do something that will keep you out of trouble. Don't follow the crowd. Of course, this can be easier said than done because you want your peers to like you. If they jumped off the tallest building in the world, would you do the same? Think about that before you do something harmful to yourself or others.

3. Use "I" statements. Communicate your feelings and needs by using "I" statements. This is a non-invasive way to give people information about yourself. State the facts and be specific. Avoid using "you always," "we never," or "I always" because this puts others on the defense. Use your statements appropriately. For example, "I want you to stop teasing me about my accent. When you do this I feel hurt." You're specific and non-judgmental.

4. Acknowledge the beliefs, feelings, and opinions of others. Believe it or not, you can agree to disagree. If everyone had the same beliefs, the world would be one-dimensional and boring. You're entitled to your opinions as are others. It's not right to impose your beliefs and opinions on others just like it's not right for them to do the same to you. Listen thoughtfully to others, and they'll do the same.

5. Act your age. If you want your parents, teachers, grandparents, etc., to treat you in an adult-like manner, act your age!

Tip 5:

What Can Self-Love Do for You?

"I remind myself to be kind to myself and as slightly ridiculous as it may sound, to treat myself in the same gentle way I'd want to treat a daughter of mine. It really helps."

- Emma Stone

Do you really want to be a winner? If you truly want to be a winner, then you must deal with self-love. Do you love yourself enough? Or does your inner critic always take over to criticize you? How can you beat this inner critic? Read on to find out!

It is easy to look down on yourself and be critical about mistakes you have made along the way. Let's consider Allison who fell in front of the whole school while climbing the stage to receive an award. This scenario never left her thoughts, and she kept criticizing herself. She was harrassed by negative thoughts and always replayed the incident mentally, imagining a better outcome.

Deanne couldn't forgive herself when she got a bad grade in math. She kept mulling it over and over in her mind, and thought she could have done better. I can relate to the experiences of both Allison and Deane because I have experienced both situations and have often looked down on myself. However, I have learned that dealing with myself this way leaves me feeling defeated, sad, and frustrated. So I literally spoke to myself and said, "Grace-Frances, you make mistakes because you are human, and everyone makes mistakes. Consider the fact that you can learn from your mistakes and do better." When I continued to repeat this to myself, I began to feel reassurred, confident, and not frustrated.

Here are a few tips to boost your self-esteem:

1. Change your negative thoughts to positive ones. Do it gradually. For example, if you made a mistake at school while taking a test, it's not the end of the world. Instead of letting your inner critic take over, take charge and say, " I will do better next time."

2. Reward yourself for the good things that you are able to do successfully. Celebrate your success with a treat of ice cream, a candy bar, or a smoothie, but more importantly, document your success in a journal such as my *Success Is A Journey, Not a Destination* motivational journal.

3. Write down four good qualities you see in yourself. Are there any bad qualities that need working on? First, focus on the good ones that you have. Be thankful for them ! Next, skim through the bad ones and be determined to work on them. Not being time conscious is a bad quality. To improve, set an alarm clock so that

you can leave home at an approriate time. Make it a habit to arrive at your destination ten minutes early. You will see a change in your timekeeping habits. Pat yourself on the back, and take on the next bad habit you want to improve. This way, you'll grow self-respect and develop confidence in yourself.

At this point in the book, write down two ways you are practicing self-love. Post it on Instagram with the hashtag #agracefulwin and tag @miss.gracefrances in your post!

How does self-love help you? Here are a few points to consider:

1. If you appreciate who you are and see good qualities in yourself, then you can appreciate and love others better.

2. If you have faith in yourself, you can confidently work on any task or project.

3. People are naturally drawn to those who exude confidence and believe in themselves. People who are self-critical and doubt themselves do not attract friends.

4. Not only does self-love impact you as a person, it impacts your community as well. Your community will appreciate the value that you bring. They will want to learn from you and find out the secret to your personality. That is why we need to work on our belief in ourselves because that is the key to our effectiveness in life. I watched a documentary on Kobe Bryant, and what I admired about him was his confidence when he first started out. He led with this confidence throughout his lifetime in basketball, and eventually, he won the heart of the world.

Tip 6:

Dealing With Procrastination

"You may delay, but time will not, and lost time is never found again."

- Benjamin Franklin

Procrastination is the habit of delaying an action when you can do it immediately. Edward Young, an English writer, coined the saying "Procrastination is the thief of time." Students often find themselves procrastinating in regard to their assignments or projects. For many students, an assignment that is due in two months is good news. They have two months to slowly work on the assignment, making necessary improvements along the way. That is how it is supposed to be done. Other students plan to get to work on that assignment, but they never get around to it. Then the due date rolls around, and that student who procrastinated is left pulling an all-nighter so that he or she can barely make the deadline the next morning. Does that sound familiar? Is this true of you?

Procrastination is not limited to the world of academia, though. Let's look at other examples outside of school. Take for instance, Lilah, who is good at braiding and would like to start her own side-hustle. Even though she is good at it, she keeps postponing and saying, "I will do it in the summer." She goes on and on, and when summer comes around, she still doesn't start. She keeps postponing and never gets it off the ground.

Martin is a good artist and wants to participate in a local art competition for the chance to win $3,000 that was announced on January 16th. The deadline for submission of artwork is May 5th. By May 2nd, Martin has not even touched a paintbrush, yet he convinces himself that he will win the prize. What is the root of all of this procrastination? It is just a problem of mindset. People are so conditioned to putting off work that after a while, it becomes a habit.

It takes discipline, desire, and willingness to address procrastination. By doing that, you would be changing the way your mind processes work.

In order to address procrastination, accept that you have a problem of procrastination, and be willing to work on it. Set timelines for deadlines that you have to meet. If you receive math homework on a Tuesday, and it is due on Thursday, work on it on Tuesday! Don't wait til the last minute.

Prioritize your tasks. Rank them from "Most Important" to "Least Important." What is due tomorrow must be done today. Don't forget to reward yourself with something tangible like a gift as you see improvement, which will serve as a reminder to keep pushing!

Tip 7:

Dealing With Self-Doubt

"The worst enemy to creativity is self-doubt."

- Sylvia Plath

Have you ever dreamt of doing something bigger than what you do every day? Have you ever wanted to start a business or write a book? Do you ever hear your inner voice saying that you are incapable of doing anything that you set out to do? Your inner voice tells you that you're not smart enough, rich enough, or creative enough. This is an experience I can relate to. We all have moments when we experience self-doubt. Even the most confident person deals with self-doubt. You can still have moments when you question your capabilities. Take a moment to consider my story and victory over self-doubt.

In 7th grade, I wanted to pursue a sport, but I was unsure of what specific sport. My first coach in middle school for track and field was Coach Sales.

I ran summer track with him in 8th grade. I had never committed to a sport before. Coach Sales believed in me and pushed me to keep running even when I doubted my abilities. My first race was the 400 meter dash. I ran my first 400 meter dash still having doubts, but I just knew I would fight to the finish. If it was not for Coach Sales, I would not have started running track in the first place. When I first started running track my freshman year of high school, I could not run a full lap during workouts. The workouts were very intense, and every day's workout was hard and draining. I started to doubt myself and wonder if track and field was the sport for me. Ironically, quitting never seemed like an option to me. I stayed the course and realized that everything is a process. I may not start out as the fastest person, but I can make tremendous improvement. My coaches made sure that they gave me the proper training to make this happen, and it was all in my mind to be successful. Every day, Coach Brittany, Coach Arielle, and Coach Mayo gave us intense workouts, and sometimes I wondered if I was getting better. I remember my first race in high school indoor track when Coach Brittany entered me in the 300 meter dash. Before entering me in the race, we discussed the ideal race to put me in, because honestly, I was not fast and did not have stamina. She said that she would recommend me for the 500 meter dash. I decided that I would run the 500 meter dash and 300 meter dash.

Fast forward to race day, I was very nervous and wondered if I made a mistake ever wanting to try. I watched all the previous races before mine and started to feel doubt because everyone seemed fast. I pushed these negative thoughts to the back of my mind and decided that if I made it this far, it would be good to continue. Before I knew it, I was on the starting line for the 300 meter dash. I was in the first lane, which is behind all the other lanes on the track. The gun went off, and I was running for my life. I started to pass all the other lanes, and surprisingly, I was the first one to cross the finish line. That was all the reassurance I needed to stick with track and field, and I made a commitment to improving every day.

At the end of my freshman year, I was awarded Girls' Most Valuable Player for Girls Track and Field. Then my sophomore year came, and I began to run cross country as well. I was able to run 3.1 miles and more when, even during my freshman year, I would not have dreamt of even doing such a thing! When I ran my first cross country race, I won the race! I was so shocked and so happy because I started seeing that track and field was for me—all I needed to do was work hard.

At the end of my sophomore year, I was awarded Girls' Most Valuable Player for Cross Country and Girls' Most Valuable Player for Indoor Track and Field. I was injured during outdoor track season for my sophomore year, but I did not give up. As soon as I recovered, I started to train again. During my junior year, I ran cross country again and hit a new achievement with my team! We became the first Girls' Cross Country team at my high school to advance to States in 19 years!

At the end of my junior year in 2020, I was awarded Girls' Most Valuable Player for Indoor Track and Field!

I owe all these achievements to my coaches who have ceaselessly empowered me. I am thankful to Coaches Brittany, Arielle, Mayo, and Sales. They provided me with the kit to be successful. All I needed was the determination to persevere.

If you have self-doubt, don't allow it to hold you back. Remember my story, I was not fast before my race, and I did not know if I was going to win or not. However, I gave it a shot, and it has made me overcome self-doubt to a great extent.

These few tips will also help.

Read books that have empowering messages. Attend events with people who share the desire to be successful. Surround yourself with people who want to see you win.

If you are unable to achieve your set goals, don't let your self-doubt overtake you. Keep trying and pushing! There will always be a light at the end of the tunnel. Today, my plaques have become reminders to me that I need not allow self-doubt to overcome me.

The journey to building something out of nothing is not paved in gold. You will have stumbling blocks along the way. When you stumble, take a step back, regroup and continue to push through.

Tip 8:

What Can You Learn From Successful People?

"The best way to be successful is to learn from other successful people."

- Martin Dai Nguyen

Being successful in life is a goal that everyone wants to achieve. In school, our teachers encourage us to aim for success. How can we achieve success? Is there a blueprint or formula for success? In fact, yes. When you want to learn to be successful at something, learn from someone who has been successful at doing that same thing.

What can you learn from successful people? The first thing that you need to do is find someone in the venture or field you intend to go into. A successful person who I admire is Oprah Winfrey. She did not let her obstacles get in the way of her goals. She had some traumatic experiences as a child. She was abused and molested by two family members and a family friend. She ran away from home at the age of 13 and at 14, had a child who later died.

Shortly after, Oprah Winfrey was awarded with a scholarship to Tennessee State University. She participated in a local beauty pageant and then became the first African-American TV correspondent in Tennessee.

At the beginning of her career, she was an evening news co-anchor, which was a huge acomplishment because at the time she was a young, black woman in the time when old, white men were making and enforcing the rules.

Then the network wanted to broaden their viewership. Oprah Winfrey was thrown into the spotlight with high demands. The show proved to be a failure, and she was blamed for it, not her co-host. She was moved down to a writing and reporting gig. This did not work out because she was a slow writer and compassionate for the content she was covering.

Oprah Winfrey did not give up, despite all of this. Instead, she took charge and kept working hard.

Much later, she moved to Chicago where she began working on her own morning show which later became known as *The Oprah Winfrey Show*.

According to *Business Insider*, Oprah Winfrey's "net worth is calculated to be about $2.6 billion, making her one of the richest black women in the world and the first female black billionaire!"

Oprah Winfrey's life path teaches me perseverance because she believed she could be successful after all the obstacles she faced.

As you research, find out about the morning routine of successful people and how they remain productive. Most successful people will have a list of books that they recommend or have read. Read these books if they apply to what you are seeking. Check to see what education they have acquired. Did they have to have specialized education or training to get to the level they're at now? Find out if they have any written material or training seminars. Learn their daily method of operation.

Most success stories are associated with some sort of "brand." Their brand will either be their name or something that they invented. Find out how they established and marketed this brand. Check to see if they outsourced a lot of their activities such as content writing, web design, marketing, and advertising. Most will have done all this for themselves when they first started, but as they became more and more successful, they found it harder and harder to do it.

As you can see, there is much to be learned from successful people. When you have the right attitude and desire to become successful, you will extract what you need to know, and if you apply what you learn, you will be well on your way to success.

Tip 9:

Keep Your Mind Open to Positive Change

"Be open-minded. You will learn more and broaden your horizon."

- Unknown

Life is filled with many possibilities—perhaps a lot more than you think. In any single day, you make hundreds if not thousands of small decisions that influence the direction of your life.

Within the past few months, I have come to believe the previous statement. Before writing this book, I did not have a clue about publishing a book. It took days of research for me to begin fomulating my own plan. If I had not kept an open mind about publishing, I would not be writing the final chapter today.

My experience with this book has taught me that opportunities truly exist. What I didn't know before about the process of publishing a book has now become a joy to me. I now enjoy creating content and researching more ways to polish my newfound craft.

In order for you to be successful, keep your mind and options open. Never say "I can't do this" or "I am not suited for this." Just give it a try! Too many times, we don't even realize all the choices and power we have in our lives.

We get so used to what is familiar, and thus we miss out on all the opportunities for positive change that pass us by constantly.

If your mind can't play with the possibility of your life taking a new direction, then you're not going to be prepared to take advantage of these opportunities when they arise.

Everyone's life is filled with opportunities, but not everyone sees them.

Conclusion

"Trust God and believe good things to come!"

- Jeffrey R. Holland

In our quest for success, we often forget that successful people had their own journeys. We tend to focus on people's accomplishments rather than the processes they had to go through. We do not pay attention to their setbacks, disappointments, humiliation, hard lessons or pain. Sometimes we may feel inadequate or even skeptical because we do not believe we can achieve as much.

Whenever you see a successful person, whether it be on Instagram or Twitter, remember that you are only witnessing the end result of their hard work. This is to say that we all have our own journey and story. Our pathways to success will not be the same, however, the principels of hard-work, perseverance, patience and commitment will apply to each and everyone of our journeys if it is worthwhile.

Have faith in your journey and trust that it is unique to you and will make you a person of purpose.

Stay focused and keep your eyes on your own journey!

Lastly, I have learned to trust God for guidance and wisdom in my everyday life. Without His guidance, I would not be writing this book today. He has seen me through my academic work and has encouraged me when I wanted to give up.

Trusting God is one of the critical aspects of being successful. Acknowledging that you cannot do it alone on your own strength will help you to put your trust in Him. Leaning on Him on a daily basis is a sure way of becoming a winner!

Taking these steps seriously will definitely lead you to the goal of being a winner!

©Grace-Frances Afful

www.ingramcontent.com/pod-product-compliance
Lightning Source LLC
Chambersburg PA
CBHW042044290426
44109CB00001B/33